Manchester Calling

Christina de la Mare

Cornelsen

Cornelsen English Library
Christina de la Mare · Manchester Calling

Verlagsredaktion
Michael Dunkel

Umschlaggestaltung
Heike Börner, Berlin

Titelbild
Konstantin Sutyagin / Shutterstock, New York

Illustration
John Batten, London

Layout
Buchgestaltung+, Berlin

Technische Umsetzung
Buch und Gestaltung, Britta Dieterle

www.cornelsen.de

1. Auflage, 1. Druck 2011

Alle Drucke dieser Auflage sind inhaltlich unverändert und können im Unterricht nebeneinander verwendet werden.

Druck: CS-Druck CornelsenStürtz, Berlin

ISBN 978-3-06-032479-8

Inhalt gedruckt auf säurefreiem Papier aus nachhaltiger Forstwirtschaft.

Contents

Chapter 1 Thursday, September 1st – Grace

It was Thursday morning, the first day back at school after the holidays. I hadn't enjoyed getting up so early, but I was happy to go back and see my friends again. The summer had been busy – I'd spent three weeks in London with my cousin Darris and his family – so I had lots to tell my friends about.

There was a girl at the bus stop that I hadn't seen before. She wore my school's uniform, so I guessed she must be a new pupil. She was older than me, about 16, but looked shy and nervous. I said hello and she smiled back, but she didn't say anything.

When we arrived at the school building she looked nervous.

"Do you want me to show you where to go?" I asked.

"I'm OK, thanks," she answered and walked towards the building. I guessed that she wasn't interested in speaking to a 13 year-old girl. I decided to forget about her and soon I was busy talking to my friends.

I saw her later in the playground. She was with a group of boys and girls. But she didn't look very happy.

After school I decided to walk home with my friends instead of taking the bus. We walked and talked together for a few minutes, then said goodbye. But then I heard somebody behind me. It was the new girl again.

This time she was friendlier. "Why aren't you on the bus?" she asked.

"I felt like walking," I answered. "What about you?"

She didn't answer, but looked around nervously. "I … err … didn't really want to talk to anybody and there were lots of people at the bus stop, so …"

"But you're talking to me," I said.

"I know," she answered. "But you're the only friendly face I've seen today."

I looked at her. She was very pretty with long brown hair. She had big gold earrings in her ears. "What did the teachers say to you about your earrings?" I asked.

"I have to take them out," she answered. "I don't like this school uniform very much – I didn't have to wear one at my old school."

The girl had an Irish accent. "Where are you from in Ireland?" I asked.

"Dublin" she answered. "I'm from a Traveller community there."

I didn't know any Travellers or Gypsies. I was sure she was the only Traveller at our school. Travellers have a bad reputation, I thought. She's going to have a hard time.

For a moment I didn't know what to say. She saw my embarrassment and said, "Do you mind walking down the road with a pikey?"

I looked at her, afraid. But she smiled at me. "No, of course I don't mind," I answered. "And my name's Grace. What's yours?"

Her smile grew wider. "It's Gina," she said.

Chapter 2 Thursday, September 29th – Gina

I was so happy that Grace lived on my street. She was more than two years younger than me, but she was clever and funny.

Grace often talked about her cousin Darris from London. He was fourteen, nearly fifteen, but looked older, she said. Grace said he was good-looking, really good at skate-boarding and really cool. I thought she had a little crush on him! Darris often came to Manchester to stay with Grace and her family. He had taught her to skateboard and sometimes they did skateboarding competitions together. I wanted to meet this cool, good-looking cousin. But there was no point, really. Dad never let me have boyfriends.

After four weeks at school, Grace was still my only friend. I felt nervous with the other kids in my class. I didn't want to tell them about myself, about where I came from. But I was sure they had guessed things about me. Girls in the class stared at my long hair and earrings. They laughed at my Irish accent. I started to hear the word "pikey" when they walked past.

I was behind the other pupils at school and I was a year older than everybody else in my class. But it wasn't my fault. After so many years on the move and so many different schools, I had missed a lot of education. I hoped that now we were in a house, I could finish school. And I wanted to work very hard.

Luckily my class teacher was nice. Her name was Mrs Jenkins and I talked to her every morning before lessons started. She understood my problems and wanted to help me. At least there was one teacher at school who believed I could do well.

So every morning I put on my school uniform, walked to school and hoped the day would go well. Every day I waited in the playground alone and checked my homework. "I'm not here to have friends," I thought. "I'm here to learn."

At least I had Grace.

I saw Grace nearly every day. Often we walked home together. I enjoyed being with her after a long day. Often I needed to ask her questions about school. It was so big – more than a thousand pupils – and there were so many rules to learn.

Grace liked asking me questions too. She wanted to know about my Irish Traveller life.

"Did you live in a caravan in Ireland?" she asked one day.

"Yes, I did." I answered. "I lived on caravan sites with my family. It was fun."

"Was it more fun than a house?" asked Grace.

"Yes," I answered, "because I was so near my cousins. It was safe for children too. We could play near the caravans when we wanted. And there were no roads on the sites."

"So why did you leave?" asked Grace, curiously.

"Well, life was hard too," I answered. "Councils don't like Irish Travellers, and they don't want you on their land. We often had to move to different sites. Things are easier now. We know we can stay in our house. My brothers and sisters and I can stay in our schools too."

That afternoon after school, I waited for Grace in the playground. Hundreds of teenagers hurried out of the school gates, but I couldn't see her anywhere. I stood in the corner of the playground and waited for her. After ten minutes everybody had gone. Maybe I've missed her, I thought, and decided to start walking home. But when I picked up my school bag I heard something behind me. I turned and saw that I wasn't alone. Three girls were staring at me, their faces hard and unfriendly.

"Pikey!" one of them said, and the others laughed. "You know we don't want people like you round here." She walked towards me. She was thin with long, dirty hair. She was small, maybe younger than me, but her face looked old and mean. Suddenly she took my bag from me and threw it to the ground. Books and papers flew out and scattered everywhere. "Oh dear," she said, "the pikey's homework!" The group of girls laughed and sneered. "But," said the girl, picking up one of the books, "this looks a bit hard for you. Pikeys can't read!"

She let the book fall to the ground again, and the group ran off, pleased with themselves. I picked up my books and put them back in my bag, then I started to walk out of the playground.

"Gina!" cried a voice.

I looked up and saw Grace running towards me.

"What happened?" she asked. "What did those girls do to you?"

"I'm OK," I said, but I didn't want to look at her.

"Gina, I know those girls," said Grace. "They're horrible. They gave me a hard time when I started at the school."

"So I'm not the only one," I said.

Slowly we walked home together.

Chapter 3 Friday, October 14th – Darris

It was Friday evening and I was on a train from London to Manchester. I yawned and stared out of the window. Rows of houses flew past me in the darkening evening.

I looked in my bag for my MP3 player and found it under my homework books. I couldn't believe Mum had packed them. I had no plans to do my homework before Sunday night, back at home in London!

I put in my earphones and sat back in my seat. My eyes closed to the sound of the music and soon I was asleep.

It seemed like only ten minutes later when the train arrived at Manchester Piccadilly station. I picked up my bag and skateboard and got off the train. The station was crowded, but I saw Grace immediately, smiling at me in her pink jacket, jeans and trainers. Grace, my sweet, funny cousin. "Hello little Gracy!" I said, and hugged her.

"Not so little!" she shouted and laughed.

Soon we were talking about our weekend: the skateboard park on Saturday, a disco at the youth club in the evening and a big Caribbean lunch at our grandma's on Sunday!

The next morning we got up late, then made a packed lunch. Then we picked up our skateboards and helmets and walked to the park near Grace's house. There was a big skateboard area, but on a warm sunny day it often got busy. As we arrived we could see that lots of other people were there too. We decided to skateboard around the park, enjoying the early autumn sunshine. After some minutes we stopped to have a drink. And then Grace started waving at somebody. It was a girl in jogging clothes.

"Gina!" she called and the girl looked towards us. She stopped running and walked over. She wore a pink T-shirt and black leggings with trainers. Her hair was in a ponytail and she was very pretty.

She stopped in front of us, looking nervous for a moment. She looked at Grace, then at me and smiled, shyly.

"This is my cousin Darris," said Grace. "He's come up from London for the weekend. Darris – this is Gina, my new friend from school. She's just moved over from Ireland."

"Hi," I said, smiling. "Sit down with us."

"I didn't know you were a runner," said Grace.

"Yes," said Gina. "It's my favourite sport. I was in an athletics club in Dublin."

"So you must be good, then," I said, looking at her.

"I am good," she said, and laughed, showing small white teeth. I looked at her for a moment, smiling.

Then I remembered Grace and looked at her. She sat with her arms crossed and looked embarrassed. I turned to Gina again.

"Do you want to come to the skateboard park with us?" I asked. "You can use my skateboard if you like."

"Err, I can't really ..." answered Gina, looking around nervously. "Well, maybe I could come – just for five minutes."

"What's the problem?" Grace asked her.

"It's my dad," she answered. "He doesn't really like me going out on my own ... and if he sees me talking to a boy, he'll be really angry!"

"But I'm here too," Grace said. "You're not alone with Darris. Come with us. It'll be fine."

"OK," she said. "But I really can't stay for long."

The three of us walked over to the skateboard park and I started to practise. It was nice to have Gina with me. She was interested too, and we talked about skateboarding, the moves, the equipment, all the competitions.

But Grace wasn't interested and after a while, she left the two of us and went to practise on her skateboard alone. I thought she was a bit angry with us, but it was so nice to be with Gina I quickly forgot about Grace again.

After an hour Gina looked at her watch. "Oh no!" she said. "It's really late. I really have to go!"

"Don't worry," I said. "We'll walk back with you, won't we, Grace. You live in the same street, don't you."

"Oh no – I can't walk with you. If my dad sees me with you, I'll be in so much trouble!" said Gina.

"Look – this is silly," I said. "We'll walk to your house with you. We'll introduce ourselves and then we'll ask if you can come to the youth club disco with us this evening. We'll explain that you won't only be with me – Grace will be there too, won't you Grace."

For a minute Grace looked really grumpy. But then she smiled and said, "Yes, of course."

"Youth club disco? Well, OK," said Gina, nervously. "But I'm telling you – just wait till you meet my dad!"

Twenty minutes later we were outside Gina's house and a very angry man with a bright red face and a heavy Irish accent glared at us.

"Where have you been?! It's been two hours, Gina! You said you wanted to run for half an hour. And who are these people? And what are they doing with you? This is the last time you go out by yourself, young lady!"

"I – I'm really sorry, Dad," she stammered. "This is Grace and her cousin Darris. Grace is at my school and she's been really kind to me. I met her and Darris in the park when I went jogging. I …"

"Excuse me, sir," I said. "I know you don't like it when your daughter goes out alone. But we only talked for a short time. And I wanted to ask if … if Gina can come to the youth club disco with us this evening."

The man looked at me, at Grace and then at Gina. His face didn't look so red. "Hmmmph," he said. "Come in."

One by one we walked into a small, clean house. We followed Gina's father through a narrow hall into a living room. It was a pretty room with nice furniture and pictures everywhere.

"Sit down," Gina's father said.

The three of us sat on a small sofa. Then her mother walked into the room.

"This is my wife Violet, and I'm Peter, Peter Ward," said her father. "What were your names again?"

We introduced ourselves and then Violet offered us some tea.

Peter sat down in a chair and looked at us.

"So, a disco, eh?" he asked, and looked at me. "You know, young man, we're from the Irish Travelling community, and we don't usually let our daughters go out with young men on their own. And we don't always let them go out with men who aren't Irish Travellers ... we like to protect the women in our community. Gina's a young girl – she doesn't know about life."

"Dad!" said Gina, and looked embarrassed.

"But you look like a nice young man – and your cousin here, she'll be with you too?"

"Yes, sir. Grace lives on this street too. So we'll bring Gina back home when the disco finishes."

"Well then. I've decided Gina can go – but on one condition. She must be home at ten o'clock."

"Aw, Dad!" said Gina. "That's so early!"

"Early, is it?" said her dad. "Well – it's that or nothing, Gina. Your choice."

"OK," said Gina sulkily.

Chapter 4 Saturday, October 15th – Grace

That evening we were at the youth club. It was crowded with teenagers and loud music. I had on jeans and a top, and Gina looked great in black leggings and a white dress. Darris wore his jeans and T-shirt as usual and stared at Gina from under his cap. I started to feel embarrassed being with the two of them, so I went to buy some drinks.

When I came back, carefully holding the drinks in my hands, Gina wasn't there and Darris was with some boys from the skateboard park. There was a lot of talk about a skateboarding competition in a few weeks' time. I touched Darris on the arm. "Where's Gina?" I asked.

"Umm … I'm not sure. I think she went to the toilets," he said, and looked around.

We waited for some minutes, but she didn't come back. Gina didn't know many people to talk to, and I started to become worried. "Hold my drink," I said to Darris. "I think I should look for her."

I looked around the club, but there was no sign of Gina. When I walked into the toilets, I heard her voice.

"Leave me alone," she said, and as I walked to the cubicles, I saw her in one of them with the three bullies from school around her. She looked really frightened.

"Pikeys aren't welcome in this club," one of the girls said. "Stay away from us. We don't want you here or at school. Go back to Ireland!"

"Get away from her!" I shouted. The girls turned and stared at me. One of them started laughing. "Do you think it's funny?" I shouted and tried to push past the girls to get to Gina. But they were bigger than me. I knew I couldn't help her on my own. I ran back through the youth club to get Darris.

"Darris!" I cried, "You have to come now! Some girls are bullying Gina in the toilets! You have to come and help her!"

Darris ran to the toilets, some of his skateboarding friends behind him. When the girls saw Darris and the other boys, they quickly ran away. Gina stood still, looking at the floor.

"Gina?" asked Darris. "Talk to me. Are you OK?"

Gina said nothing for a few seconds. Then she looked up at Darris. "I want to go home," she said, sadly.

The three of us walked home. I had my arm around Gina. She was taller than me, but she felt frail and small. Darris walked next to us. Nobody said anything.

Then, outside her house, Gina turned to us. "I'm fine now," she said. "You don't have to come in with me."

The front door opened and her mother came out. "You OK, love?" her mother asked.

"I'm fine, Mum!" said Gina and hurried into the house. Before she disappeared she turned to us again and whispered, "Thanks for your help!"

Then she was gone.

After we took Gina home, Darris and I stayed up late to read about Irish Travellers on the Internet. We knew nothing about them and now that Gina was our friend we wanted to know much more.

We learned that Irish Travellers are probably from 12th century Ireland, when many people lost their homes and land. The Travellers started to earn money by travelling around the country. A strong Traveller community developed with its own language, Shelta. Irish Travellers are now called an ethnic minority in the UK because they share a culture and language. Irish Travellers sometimes move around the country, but they don't always want to. There isn't enough land for their caravans, and councils don't let them stay in one place. For this reason, many Irish Traveller children don't spend enough time at school.

There was lots of interesting information on the Internet. But there were some really horrible, racist comments about Irish Travellers too. It was like reading about racism against black people fifty years ago. How could people have this attitude in the 21st century? Darris and I thought about our friend. And we wanted to help her.

The next morning we knocked on Gina's door. Her mother Violet answered it and called Gina. When Gina came to the door she looked pleased to see us.

She waited till her mother had gone again and said, "Thanks for helping me last night. I need bodyguards like you!"

We all laughed and then Darris said, "I'm going back to London in a few hours, but I hope we can see each other again the next time I come to Manchester."

"I'd like that," said Gina. "Maybe you can come to my house and my mum will cook, or something."

"I'll see you soon," said Darris.

"Darris," said Gina, "Here, I want to give you something." She gave him a small piece of paper. "It's my mobile number," she said. "Text me."

Chapter 5 Friday, November 4th – Gina

The next time Darris came to Manchester, things were very different.

I knew there was a skateboarding competition that weekend and that Darris wanted to be in it. We had texted each other a lot over the last few weeks, but now I really wanted to talk to him about it. But I couldn't. We had visitors from Ireland, and I had to be there to look after them and talk to them.

Our visitors were from Dad's side of the family: his cousin Mary, her mother and her son Robert. Robert was the reason they were in our house. Aged 20, Robert wanted to get married, and he was interested in me.

Dad thought it was great. Robert and his father had a successful business in Ireland. In Dad's eyes, Robert was the perfect husband!

But Robert wasn't ... really what I wanted. He was good-looking. He was quite funny too – sometimes. But he was terribly arrogant. He spent a lot of money on clothes, and I knew he had a nice car because he often talked about it, but he wasn't interested in the same things as me. More importantly, I didn't think he was very interested in me! He didn't want to know about my life in Manchester, my school work or my plans for the future. I knew he wanted a good little wife, not a wife with an education. He wanted a wife who spent all day cleaning his caravan and who could give him lots of sons and daughters.

It was not what I wanted. But Dad loved Robert. And because Dad was the head of our family, I had to make him happy.

I missed Darris. He was so funny, and I felt that we had lots in common. I sat at my bedroom window and looked across the street to Grace's house.

Then suddenly, their front door opened and Darris came out with Grace behind him. What are they doing? I wondered. Then they walked towards our house! Oh no! I thought.

They knocked on the door. I heard Robert go to answer it. Why is he going? I thought, crossly. It isn't his house!

I heard the door open and then Darris' voice.

"Hi," said Darris, "I wanted to ..."

"Yeah?" Robert said. "What did you want?"

"I want to see Gina," said Darris.

"Why?" asked Robert.

"She's a friend," said Darris.

"She isn't here," said Robert.

Then I heard Dad go to the door. This is getting bad! I thought.

"You mustn't come here anymore, Darris. Gina doesn't want to see you," said Dad.

"But – Mr Ward, I ...," said Darris, sounding confused.

"I'm telling you, son. Things are different now. She doesn't ... want ... to see you. Now go before I get angry."

The front door closed.

I watched as Darris marched across the road. He looked angry and upset. And I felt the same.

Chapter 6 Saturday, November 5th – Darris

The next morning I woke up and immediately felt sad. For a moment I couldn't understand why. Then I remembered Gina's dad and her horrible new boyfriend Robert.

Grace had explained everything about Gina and this new man in her life. It sounded bad to me. We were in the 21st century. Fathers don't pick their daughters' husbands any more! I thought. But then I remembered. Gina was an Irish Traveller, and for her things had to be different.

I had thought we could still be friends. I felt really angry with her dad. I stared at my cornflakes, but I couldn't eat.

At least I had another great love in my life – my skateboard. I managed to eat some breakfast, and then I got dressed and picked up my skateboard. I went outside to Grace's back garden and practised some moves.

I had entered a competition at the skateboard park near Grace's house. Lots of people wanted to be in it. I felt really excited about it and wanted to show people what I could do.

For me, my skateboard was like an extra leg or arm. I never wanted to be without it. I had got my first skateboard on my fifth birthday, and from that day I had been in love with skateboarding.

I had practised for years, and I could do lots of different tricks. My favourite style of skateboarding was vert skateboarding. In vert skateboarding you skateboard on a ramp in the shape of a U. As you skate down and then up the ramp your skateboard moves faster, and when you get to the top you and your board fly up into the air. This is when you do your tricks. They're called *airs*.

That afternoon, Grace and I walked over to the skateboard park for the competition.

I couldn't wait to start.

There were three rounds in the competition, so each skateboarder had three chances to show how good he or she was. In the first round I did some good airs. But in the second round I fell off my board. Luckily I had all the correct safety equipment, including a skateboarding helmet and the right shoes.

In the third round I did my highest air. I felt fantastic.

After the competition I was really hungry, so Grace and I went to a burger bar and bought some food. We walked home, talking, eating and laughing. For a while, at least, it was nice not to think about Gina.

Chapter 7 Saturday, November 5th – Grace

Darris didn't win the competition. "And I don't mind," he said. "I'm just pleased that I was there. It was great!"

Darris loved being outside and doing sport. He wanted a career in it, but he wasn't sure what he wanted to do.

"What are you going to do when you leave school, Darris?" my grandma always asked him. "You have to work hard and get a good job!"

Darris knew all this. "I work hard, Grandma!" he always said, smiling. "I know what I want to do when I leave school. I'm going to go to college to study sport. I'm going to do something I love!"

That night was Bonfire Night. At six o'clock we went out into the wintry evening air. Darris, Mum, Grandma and I walked together to the park to watch a firework display.

As the fireworks flew up into the sky, the crowd oohed and aahed. I looked at their smiling faces. Then I looked at Darris. He looked very serious.

That night we sat in his bedroom and listened to rap music. After a while I felt tired and went to my bedroom to read. But before I got in to bed I went to my window to look out into the street. The night was dark and cold, but I could see Gina in her front garden with Robert and her mother. Robert said something, then laughed loudly – but Gina didn't look very impressed. Does she like Robert? I wondered.

The next day, as we drove Darris to the station, he talked about Gina for the first time in two days. "Maybe I should invite her to a skateboard competition," he said, smiling. "Then she'll see how good I am and forget about Robert."

But we knew that life was never that simple.

Chapter 8 Sunday, November 6th – Gina

I liked our house the first time I saw it. It was small, nothing special from the outside, but inside it was clean with freshly painted walls and nice carpets. We had only been there a few months, but already, it looked like a real home. My mum had filled it with our furniture, ornaments and photos. In our bedrooms the walls were covered with posters. The girls' beds were covered with dolls, teddies and pretty cushions. And my brother's bed was littered with toys.

It had been more than a week since Robert's arrival and he had started to annoy me.

"Can't they go to a hotel or something?" I asked my mum one day as we stood in the garden. "We only have a little house, and it's getting so crowded."

Mum looked through the window to the living room. Robert's grandmother sat in a big chair in front of the TV. All she did every day was watch TV. She was always in a bad mood about something. And I was sure that she didn't like me! On the sofa sat Robert and his mother with cups of tea. Their fifth cup of tea that morning. But they never made the tea, oh no! It was always Mum or me. There was no room for us in our own living room. And Robert never let go of the remote control – we couldn't pick our own programmes any more. Go home! I thought.

"A hotel?" asked Mum, and started laughing. "Have you suddenly become all hoity-toity, young lady? We can't send them away, Gina. They're family!"

I sighed and looked around the garden. "I'm not sure about Robert, Mum. We aren't really interested in the same things. He's nice, and good-looking … and funny … but he thinks I should leave school. I don't want to leave school!"

"I know," answered Mum. "But he could give you a nice life, love. He and his dad are doing really well with their business. And back in Ireland you'll be near all our family again. And it would make your dad so happy … of course …"

"I want to find my own husband," I said, starting to feel frustrated.

"And you can, of course you can," said Mum gently. "But give Robert a chance."

We heard somebody behind us and turned around. There was Robert.

"Hello ladies!" he said. "Any chance of something to eat, Gina?" he asked. "It's nearly 12 o'clock and I'd love a bacon sandwich!"

"The bacon's in the kitchen!" I snapped at him. "I'm sure you know how to make it yourself!" I left him and Mum in the garden and walked back into the house.

I felt really angry. Robert and his mum and grandma had taken over our house. I decided to escape for a while and go for a run.

I got changed into my running clothes quickly. But when I got to the front door, Robert was there.

"Is something wrong?" he asked, looking at me.

"No," I answered, looking at the floor.

"Where are you going?" he asked.

"For a run," I answered, crossly.

"What now? But it's 12 o'clock. Stay and make us something to eat. We can go for a little walk later."

"I don't want to …" I started, then gave up. "OK," I said.

I got changed again, then went into the kitchen to make bacon sandwiches for everybody. I gave Robert his sandwich first, and he took a large bite. "A bit burnt!" he said.

I sighed.

Chapter 9 Monday, November 7th – Darris

Hi Gina,

It's me again. I hope you don't mind if I e-mail you. I'm sorry that I couldn't see you at the weekend. But I know things are different now. Grace has told me that Robert is your boyfriend. She told me that you're also planning to get married. I just hope we can be friends.

I'm writing to you from my room at home. It's at the top of an old house in Brixton. Do you know Brixton? It's a great part of London – really lively and full of culture. There's a really cool music scene here, and I go to a lot of concerts.

School was really tough today. Maths and English – my worst subjects! I can't wait to leave school. Only another year and a few months. Do you feel the same? I don't want to be a schoolboy any more. I want to be in the big wide world and get a job! Something to do with sport. I'm not sure what, yet, but I'll know soon.

Whatever I choose to do, I know I have to study, so I should stop writing to you and do some homework.

But Gina, I just want to say, I think you know what you want in life. You're strong and determined, like me. I hope you get what you want because you deserve it.

Lots of love,

Darris

Chapter 10 Monday, November 7th – Grace

Gina and I usually walked to school together, but on Monday morning she didn't knock on my door. She's avoiding me, I thought. I left the house and walked quickly down the road. I soon saw her – about 100 metres in front. I ran to catch up with her. When she saw me, she didn't stop or smile, but carried on walking.

"Why don't you say hello?" I asked. "I haven't seen you all weekend."

"Sorry," she said, and smiled. "It's just … things are a bit hard now."

"I do understand a bit … I guess you don't want to see Darris again," I said.

"It's not that – I really like Darris, but, you know … Robert is here now and you know that my family are making plans for us."

"Are you going to get married?" I asked. "Wow – it's so old-fashioned – your family are arranging your future for you!"

"Well, that's how Irish Travellers do it. My dad wants it that way, and I don't have a choice." Gina looked a bit angry.

"Do you like Robert?" I asked.

"Yes, he's nice," she answered, but she didn't sound very sure.

"And does he like you?" I asked.

"I think so," she replied. "But he doesn't like my meals! A good Irish Traveller wife needs to cook good food!"

Then she stopped and looked at me. "Grace," she said. "I need you to help me."

Oh no! I thought. What is she going to ask me to do?

She took an exercise book out of her bag. “It’s my history homework,” she continued. “I’ve done it right, but my spelling is terrible. Could you look at it? I don’t need it till tomorrow.”

What a relief! I thought. Spelling was one thing I could do right.

“No problem, Gina,” I said. “I’ll give it back to you this evening.”

Chapter 11 Saturday, November 12th – Grace

The weekend came. I got up on Saturday morning, looked at my clothes and sighed. I had nothing nice to wear. Just jeans, jeans … more jeans … and T-shirts. "I dress like a boy!" I said. I wanted to wear something pretty. I needed to go shopping. But what with? I didn't have any money!

I looked at my mum's car outside on the street. It needed a clean. I ran to look for my mother.

"Mum, Mum!" I called. "If I clean your car, will you pay me some money? I really want to go shopping. I don't have any nice clothes!"

Mum looked at me and smiled. "OK," she said. "But do a good job!" Then she took twenty pounds out of her bag and put them in my hand.

"Twenty pounds? Mum, are you sure?"

"You're a good girl, Grace," she said. "Spend it wisely!"

Outside I cleaned the car in warm water and listened to music on my MP3 player. A Beyoncé track came on, and I started dancing a bit as I cleaned the car. Nobody was in the street, so nobody could see me – or so I thought, as I danced and sang to myself.

"If you liked it then you should have put a ring on it," sang Beyoncé and I together. I hopped from foot to foot and spun around.

"Oi!" shouted a man as I crashed into him with my bucket. Water flew everywhere – all over his expensive jeans and jacket.

"Watch what you're doing!" he shouted. I knew the Irish accent. I looked up and there in front of me was Robert, very wet and very angry.

"I'm s-sorry!" I said. "Can I get you a towel for your clothes?"

"No," he snapped, walking away. "But you could get a pair of glasses!"

Well, I thought. He's rude! I finished cleaning the car and went into the house.

After lunch I took the bus into town. I had twenty-seven pounds, and I couldn't wait to start spending it. I went into my favourite shop and started looking at the clothes.

"What are you looking for?" said a voice I knew. In front of me was Gina and her little sister Rosie. I smiled and said, "Everything! All I can buy for twenty-seven pounds! But I don't know where to start!"

"Let me help you," said Gina, and we started looking together. Rosie looked too. In a few minutes we had lots of clothes to take to the changing room. We had great fun trying on clothes together.

"No, too dark!" said Gina, when I put on a black dress.

"Too big!" I said, when Gina put on a pair of jeans.

"Perfect!" we said to Rosie, as she tried on a red dress. "You look beautiful!"

Little Rosie smiled happily.

At the end of our shopping trip Gina had two new dresses and a jacket, Rosie had the red dress and some jeans, and I had a beautiful jacket and a new pair of leggings. I felt very pleased with my clothes.

We had a few pounds left so we went to a burger bar. We sat next to the window and looked at our new clothes.

"I had an e-mail from Darris a few days ago," said Gina. "But I had to read it when Robert wasn't there. He'll be angry if he sees it."

"Did Robert tell you I threw water all over him?" I asked.

"Yes," she said, laughing. "It was so funny. He was so angry about that stupid jacket. It was new and really expensive! But he shouldn't spend so much money on clothes!"

I really wanted to ask Gina about Darris' e-mail, but I knew it was private. I just felt a bit worried. I was worried about Gina, but I was worried about Darris too. He was my favourite person in the whole world, and I hated it when he was upset. But I realised that they had feelings for each other. I couldn't get involved. The two of them had to solve their problems on their own.

Chapter 12 Monday, November 14th – Grace

On Monday, it was raining, so Gina and I travelled on the bus to school. I checked her homework again.

"Your spelling is getting better," I said. Gina looked pleased.

"There's a writing competition at school," she said. "I think I'm going to enter it."

"Do it, Gina!" I said. "That's great! And you know I'll help you with the spelling."

Gina looked happy and relaxed. Robert and his family had gone back to Ireland that day. Maybe that was the reason why.

"But they'll be back here for Christmas," she said.

Darris will be here for Christmas too, I thought. What will happen?

Christmas was great fun in our family. We usually spent it in Manchester because my grandmother was here. Our house was bigger too. When Darris and his family came to visit, our house was full of people and noisy, but I loved it.

Jamaican people also celebrate Christmas on the 25th, but they prepare their food the day before, on Christmas Eve. That's what we did in our house. In our family, we always ate traditional Jamaican Christmas food. For breakfast, we ate a special fruit called ackee – it tastes like eggs! I hated it, but I always tried a little bit because it made my grandmother happy. We always ate the ackee with fish and drank fruit juice. Then, later in the day, we had another traditional meal – this time, chicken and ham – I liked that meal better! And there was a fruit cake – I liked that too.

And of course, there were presents. And Father Christmas! Darris and I didn't believe in him any more, of course, but we still hung our stockings up at the ends of our beds on Christmas Eve. In the morning they were always full!

"How do you spend Christmas?" I asked Gina at school one day.

"Like most people," she answered. "Stockings up on Christmas Eve, church on Christmas morning, then presents, then an enormous Christmas dinner!"

"At least you don't have to eat fish for breakfast!" I said, and we laughed.

Chapter 13 Saturday, November 19th – Gina

It was Saturday morning. A day of relaxation for many – a day when people could get up late, watch TV, go shopping. But not for me! Not in the Ward house!

Dad was at work. Mum had taken my brother and sisters swimming. And I had to clean the house – from top to bottom!

In Irish Traveller families, girls learn to do housework when they're young. And when I say housework, I mean everything: they have to clean the kitchen, bathroom, hall, living room and bedrooms. They have to clean the windows, take out the rubbish, wash and iron the clothes, and put them away! We only had a small house, but I believed it was the cleanest house in Manchester. Dad often said that in our home, you could eat your dinner off the floor!

After years of practice, I was really good at cleaning. Now it only took me a morning. But when I finished, there was more to do – I had to do my homework!

So there I was, cloth in hand, cleaning the kitchen, somebody knocked at the door. It was Grace.

"Time for a cup of tea?" she asked.

"OK," I answered. "But I haven't finished cleaning yet."

Grace looked around. "You're fantastic Gina," she said. "I don't do as much around the house. I only wash up after dinner."

"Well, it's normal in Irish Traveller families." I said. "Girls learn to clean when they're young. I think it's a good thing. When I'm older and married, I'll always have a nice clean home. If I go back to Ireland," I said, and stopped. "If I go back to Ireland ... then Rosie will start doing the cleaning. She's ready to start learning too."

"People need to know more about Irish Travellers," said Grace.

I rinsed my cloth in hot water, then started to clean the cooker.

"They do," I replied. "But tell that to those girls at school who call me a dirty pikey."

Chapter 14 Tuesday, December 13th – Darris

Grace was on the phone. She had some news. "Gina and Robert are engaged," she said.

I had expected it, but still I felt shocked. Now there was no chance for me and Gina.

"I'll have to forget about her now," I said.

"That'll be hard," said Grace. "You'll be here in a few days."

She was right. Christmas was around the corner, and soon I would be with Grace and her family in Manchester, only a few metres from Gina's home.

Later I sent Gina a text message. "Congratulations" it said. She didn't reply, but she didn't need to. After all, there was nothing to say.

Chapter 15 The week before Christmas – Grace

School finished on December 16th, and Darris wasted no time in coming up to Manchester. His mum, dad and sister planned to travel up by car a few days later. But Darris couldn't wait. He wanted to see his friends at the skateboard park again and to practise some new tricks. If he wanted to see Gina, he didn't say it.

That evening, as we sat alone in the living room, he came clean.

"Gina has e-mailed me," he said. "She misses me, and she isn't sure about Robert. I'm hoping, really hoping that she's going to finish with him."

I didn't answer, but looked around the room. Decorations and Christmas cards were on the walls. A spicy smell of Christmas cake lingered in the air.

"Well, I hope things go well for you, Darris," I said.

That night snow started to fall, and by the following morning, the street and houses were white. I started to feel really happy about Christmas.

Town was busy and the shops were full as people used the last few shopping days to buy presents for friends and family.

At home Mum cleaned everything to prepare for our visitors over Christmas. Grandma worried about the food and checked her Christmas fruit cake every five minutes.

I cleaned my bedroom and prepared a bed for Darris' sister Faye. She was 13, like me. We liked each other and were good friends.

Every morning we got up late and had a big family breakfast. Then Darris, Faye and I ran outside to throw snowballs at each other and make snowmen. We had a competition to see who could build the biggest, best, snowman. Darris' was the best. It was enormous and wore his baseball cap.

A few days before Christmas, Darris' dad went to buy a Christmas tree and that evening the whole family decorated it. We talked about where to put the decorations until the tree was so full of them it looked ready to fall over! We were all so busy with Christmas, we all forgot about Gina. Until the night of December 23rd, when Darris crept out of the door late at night.

Faye and I had no idea what he was doing. The whole family was asleep when Darris crept across the road and waited outside Gina's house. Soon her front door opened and Gina came out, closing the door behind her as quietly as she could. The two held each other for a long time and whispered to each other, full of all the things they wanted to say.

Then they crept back to their houses as quietly as they could. But somebody saw them as they walked back through their front doors.

Chapter 16 Saturday, Christmas Eve – Grace

Darris told me what he did yesterday. He was really happy. He believed that he and Gina could be together one day. But about an hour later, somebody knocked loudly on the door, and then Robert and Gina's dad marched into the house. They wanted to see Darris. They wanted to tell him to leave Gina alone.

"What do you think you're doing, talking to my girlfriend in the middle of the night?!" asked Robert furiously, standing taller than Darris and too close for comfort.

I could see what Darris wanted to say to Robert, but he didn't want to make trouble for Gina. So he stood quietly in the hall and said nothing. Gina's father's face was bright red. He pointed at Darris.

"I told you before to leave her alone!" he shouted. "And now I'm telling you this: Robert is her fiancé, and you are not welcome in my house any more. Stay away from my daughter!"

Darris' father walked into the hall.

"Excuse me," he said, "but what is going on here? What has my son done to make you so angry?"

"You sir," cried Gina's father, "need to teach your son a few things. The two of them were out on the street in the middle of the night, talking. Tell him that it is not the right way to behave. Not with a girl who is engaged to be married!"

The two men marched out of the house. Darris' father closed the door and looked at Darris. "I think you'd better tell me what's going on," he said.

In the living room, Darris told him everything. That he and Gina really liked each other, that they had things in

common and the same goals for the future – they both wanted to do well at school. They were both interested in a career in sport. That she was beautiful. And that he just couldn't stop thinking about her. Then he said that Gina was an Irish Traveller. That meant that she had to have an Irish Traveller husband. And that Robert – the angry young man in the hall – was her fiancé.

Darris told his dad about all the e-mails and text messages between him and Gina. He said that Gina wasn't allowed to see him any more. Now he and Gina could only meet in secret. So they had met in the street in the middle of the night.

Chapter 17 Sunday, Christmas Day – Gina

Christmas in our house was noisy, but Robert and my dad didn't speak to me all day. That was fine by me because I didn't want to speak to them.

Dad had shouted at me for ages the night before. He had shouted so much I had stopped listening. Now he and Robert sat and talked to each other and occasionally gave me dirty looks. Robert's mother and grandmother did the same. I decided to ignore all of them. There was enough to do: the turkey, the kids, the endless cups of tea and all the new toys and wrapping paper all over the floor.

My favourite present was a pair of boots from Mum. She knew I wanted them. There were presents from the kids too: pretty earrings and some hand lotion. There were also presents from Dad and Robert and his family, but I hadn't opened them. I wanted to open them when it was quieter.

The row the night before had changed something. I didn't feel frightened of my dad any more, only angry. He wanted to control my life, but I didn't think he knew or cared what I really felt. And Robert? He was lazy and ignorant. I was sure I didn't want to be with him.

From now on I was going to carry on with things that were important to me: help Mum, look after my brother and sisters, do my homework and write my story for the writing competition. Nothing else mattered.

But there was something else that was important. My relationship with Darris. At that moment I wasn't sure what to do. I couldn't go to his house – I was too embarrassed. And maybe he was angry with me. I didn't know. But, whatever the situation, the only thing I could do was wait.

Chapter 18 Sunday, Christmas Day – Darris

The whole family knew about Gina. I didn't want Grandma to know, but it was unavoidable. She had been in our house when Gina's dad and Robert had come over! Gina's dad had shouted so loudly, I think the whole street knew our business now. Mum and Dad were worried about me. They were angry too. "You shouldn't be involved with Gina: she's engaged!" said Mum. But I knew that they felt sorry for me as well.

On Christmas morning, everybody decided that Gina was a banned subject for the day. We wanted to enjoy the day together and only think about nice, happy things. It wasn't too hard to do that. When Grace, Faye and I woke up that morning and found our stockings full of presents, we were as happy as three little children, laughing and shouting as we pulled out present after present. And then, after breakfast the real fun started. The family sat around the tree and took turns to give presents to each other. My present to Grace was a bracelet. My little cousin was older now, and I knew she wasn't such a tomboy any more. She loved skateboarding, but she was beginning to appreciate more feminine things too. When I saw the smile on her face, I knew she liked the gift.

Grace's present to me was a really nice T-shirt. And from Mum and Dad there were more clothes and some money. Then it was grandma's turn to give out gifts. But her presents weren't under the tree. She gave me an envelope. In it was a cheque – for a lot of money. "For college," she said, and smiled. "You're going to need it."

I threw my arms around her. "Thanks, Grandma," I said. "But it's too much!"

"Not for Darris, my clever boy with a fantastic future in front of him," she said. "Put it in a bank and save it. And when the time comes, use it wisely!"

Chapter 19 Wednesday, December 28th – Gina

My hand ached. I put down my pen and stared at the hundreds of words on the page. I had guessed the spelling of most of the words, but that no longer mattered. My story was nearly finished, and I knew that Grace wanted to check it for me. This piece of writing meant everything. I really didn't care whether or not I won the competition now. What was much more important was that people read what I had to say, that people understood.

Downstairs my brother and sisters banged their toys and shouted. Mum tried to stop them, but she was busy with the housework. It was time to go and help.

"I'll tell you what, Gina," Mum said, leaning against the cooker with my youngest sister in her arms. "I'm fed up with our visitors." I looked through the doorway into the living room. Robert, his mother and grandmother were in their usual positions in front of the TV. Tea cups lay at their feet. Magazines were scattered across the floor. And Robert's hand lay possessively over the remote control.

I walked back into the kitchen. "Four more days, Mum," I said. "Then they'll be gone."

"Take this bag of rubbish outside, Gina," said Mum, giving it to me. I carried it down the hall and opened the front door. Outside it was cold and sunny. As I put the rubbish in the bin, Grace and Darris came out of the house. They were followed by more people who looked like their family. They laughed and talked as they walked down the road. I wonder where they're going, I thought.

Back inside I suddenly felt claustrophobic. I couldn't bear another minute in the little house with too many people in it. "Mum, is it OK if I go out?" I asked. "I'll take Rosie with me."

Mum saw the look on my face. "Will you take Lucy too?" she asked, looking down at my youngest sister. Lucy smiled up at me. Two years old, she was sweet and full of fun, but she wore my mother out.

"OK," I said, and took Lucy's little hand. I called to Rosie, and we put on our coats, found Lucy's pushchair and rushed out of the house before Robert and his mum could ask for another bacon sandwich.

Chapter 20 Wednesday, December 28th – Darris

It was a beautiful day and great to be outside. Me, Grace, Faye, Mum, Dad and Grandma strolled down the road together. We went to our favourite Italian restaurant for lunch.

In the restaurant Grandma beamed as she looked at us. "My lovely family," she said happily. "It's so lovely to have you all with me."

As a family we were close – London was far from Manchester – but we spent a lot of time together. This was a good thing, of course. I knew that many families didn't have as much contact, but sometimes I felt that my grandma, aunts and uncles knew too much about my life. I felt that I deserved more privacy, and as grandma turned to look at me and frowned, I felt the need for privacy even more!

"Darris," she said, her voice cutting through the noise of eating and drinking. "I'm worried about you."

Oh no, I thought. Not here!

"That girl," she said, "Gina. Her family will cause you trouble." She leaned across the table and took my hand in hers. "A good-looking boy like you, there are so many girls out there!"

I was starting to feel angry and wanted to say something when I looked at her hand over mine. It was frail and thin and I remembered that she was an old lady, an old lady who deserved respect.

I looked at Dad, who raised a finger to his lips. "Maybe you're right, Grandma," I said, and smiled.

After lunch we decided to go for a walk in the park. The sun was still bright in the sky, but it was windy, and the temperature had dropped by a few degrees.

In the park the snow had started to disappear, but a few children were making snowballs with the dirty grey snow that remained, throwing them at their friends and laughing. But when the sun disappeared behind a cloud, the park quickly emptied. Then I heard a child's scream, and a toddler started to cry. Dad and I looked at each other, then ran towards the sound. Through some trees we saw a little girl crying in her pushchair, a young girl kneeling and crying, and a few yards away a group of teenage girls around somebody. Dad and I shouted and ran towards them. As they turned and ran I recognized their faces. And on the ground, I recognized their victim immediately. It was Gina.

She lay on the floor, her eyes were swollen shut, and she cried in pain. I took off my jacket and put it over her. Dad called an ambulance. And then Mum, Fay, Grace and Grandma came through the trees and saw what had happened. They ran to Gina's sisters and tried to comfort them.

Chapter 21 Wednesday, December 28th – Gina

I had a cracked rib and two black eyes. I had to stay in hospital, so that the doctors could watch me. I was only allowed three visitors, but my parents and all my brothers and sisters were there, as well as Robert, his mother and grandmother.

Everybody wanted to know what happened. I had forgotten nearly everything, but Rosie, poor Rosie, remembered every detail. How the girls had appeared from nowhere. How they had frightened poor Lucy, making her cry, and how they had pushed me to the ground and started to kick me. I didn't know how Darris had found me, but I was happy, so happy that he had, in more ways than one. Because of Darris, my injuries weren't so bad. Maybe now my dad could accept him.

I felt safer too. I knew my attackers, and Darris had also seen them. The police had our stories, and now they were at the homes of the girls. Maybe life will be a bit easier now, I thought.

The worst injury was to my rib. It hurt so much! Every time I breathed I felt a sharp pain. And talking was difficult too. I was relieved when a nurse came and told us there were too many people round my bed. One by one my family left, but Mum stayed by my side and held my hand.

"Gina," she said and looked at me sadly. "When did the bullying start?"

"In September," I whispered. I couldn't look at her. Instead I stared out of the window.

"But you never told us!" said Mum. I knew that she had started to cry. "Why didn't you say anything?"

There were so many reasons why. Because it wasn't the first time I had been bullied. Because I thought I was strong enough to fight it on my own. Because Mum was always so busy and so tired. Because I didn't want to make her sad.

I felt ashamed for not saying anything. Mum thought I didn't trust her. And now she felt she had let me down. "I'm sorry," I whispered.

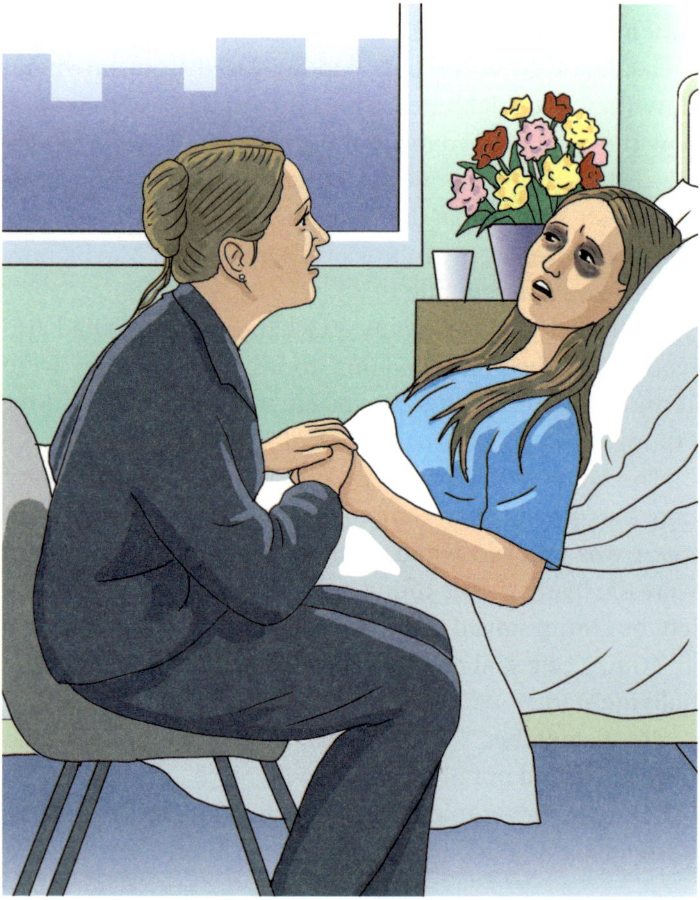

Chapter 22 Thursday, December 29th – Grace

I watched as Gina's dad parked outside their house. First he got out of the car, then Gina's mum, and then the two of them helped Gina to get out of the car. She moved very slowly, walking between her parents up to their front door. Robert opened it, and she went in.

"She's home," I said to Darris, who was sitting on the floor behind me, playing a computer game.

Darris said nothing. In a few days he was returning to London. Maybe he would never see Gina again. He had saved her from a serious injury. Maybe he had even saved her life, but nothing had changed. There was no word from her or her family.

Chapter 23 Saturday, December 31st – Gina

"Oww!" I shouted as Robert threw himself on the sofa next to me. I could sit on the sofa with cushions around me, but every movement was painful. "Sorry!" he said and picked up the newspaper. "Let's see what's on TV."

Mum and Dad came in, carrying cups of tea. Mum gave one cup to me and sat down.

Dad and Robert had decided to speak to me again. With my cracked rib and my two black eyes, they couldn't be angry with me any more. But I still felt angry with them. I spoke to them when I had to, otherwise I avoided conversation. But now I had no choice.

"Will you miss me when I go back?" asked Robert, smiling with his mouth wide open. He had a sandwich, and I could see bits of it on his tongue. I looked away quickly. "What time is your flight tomorrow?" I asked.

"So the answer's yes!" said Robert and looked at my dad and laughed.

Robert ate some more of his sandwich and chewed it loudly. Then he looked at my dad and said, "So, you'll keep Gina away from that idiot across the road!" Dad opened his mouth to answer, but this time it was my mother who spoke first.

"That boy," she said, standing up and looking angrily at Robert, "is not an idiot. He has a name, and it's Darris. Darris saved my daughter's life!" She was angry now and her voice became louder. "He is a nice boy. I've met him and talked to him. He is polite and helpful, and he has been good to Gina." I was shocked. Mum was furious. I had never seen her like this before. I looked at Dad. Even he looked frightened!

Mum wasn't finished. "If Gina goes to Ireland with you, she'll lose everything. After all that education, all her hard work, she'll have no qualifications. But she wants a career, an exciting future! And I want that for her too! That boy across the road, 'that idiot', as you call him, wants the same things as Gina. He's good for Gina. And I'm telling you, Peter," she said, now pointing at my dad, "If Darris ever comes to our house again, he will be welcome here."

Dad said nothing, only looked at the floor. Then slowly he stood up and left the room.

Chapter 24 Sunday, January 1st – Darris

There was a knock at the door. I stopped packing my bag for a minute to see who it was. Looking down the stairs I watched my dad open the door. Then I saw a look of surprise on his face.

"May I come in for a minute?" asked an Irish voice I recognized. I was shocked as Gina's dad walked into the hall. "I'd like to wish you and your family a Happy New Year," he said, "and I'd like to speak to Darris."

The two men looked at each other for a few seconds. Then my dad said, "Please, come in and sit down."

They disappeared into the living room. I crept down the stairs and stood by the door to the living room, watching them through the gap in the door.

"You know that I'm angry with Darris," Gina's dad said. "He should know better. My daughter is engaged, as you know."

My dad said nothing, but waited.

"Irish Travellers are proud people," Gina's dad continued. "We're proud of our culture. That's why I hope that Gina will marry Robert, another Irish Traveller." He stopped talking and looked at the floor, breathing deeply.

"But," he said, "I know that Darris has done a lot for my daughter. He's saved her from serious injury." Now he looked ready to cry! "A-and, I'd like to thank him."

Gina's dad sat back in his chair, looking exhausted. Now it was my dad's turn to speak.

"We understand how you feel," he said. "We've talked to Darris, and he knows he has done wrong. And I appreciate that you've come here. I'll get him for you."

Dad stood up and walked to the door. "Ah," he said, as he found me behind it, "Here he is. Come in, Darris."

I walked in and walked over to Gina's father.

"Hello Mr Ward," I said nervously.

"Darris," he said, without smiling. "You know I'm not happy with your behaviour." He stood up. "But you saved my daughter." He took my hand and shook it. "I want to thank you." Then he sat down again.

"I also think," he carried on, "that Gina would like to see you. She's, err … very fond of you. So, if you want to come to our house, you're welcome."

"Thank you," I said. Then nobody said anything. Nobody knew what to say.

"I should go," said Gina's dad, and stood up quickly. We followed him to the front door.

"Thank you for coming," my father said. "We appreciate it. Oh, and Happy New Year!"

We watched as Gina's father walked back to his house. Things suddenly felt very different.

Chapter 25 Saturday, January 14th – Grace

Gina couldn't go back to school at the start of term, but I visited her often, talked to her about school and helped her with her story. When she felt better she started to go out for short walks, and that Saturday she sat in our living room, still a bit sore, but very happy.

She wasn't only there to see me. Next to her on the sofa sat Darris, holding her hand with a grin from ear to ear.

How things had changed! Robert had gone back to Ireland. "Forever, I hope!" Gina said. She had talked to her father too. Finally he realised how unhappy she had been. When she had told him that she and Robert had split up, he hadn't said anything.

Gina and Darris were finally a couple. They texted each other every day, talked on the phone and even talked about their future together!

Darris wanted to come to Manchester as often as he could. Gina wanted to stay with him in London too, but every time she talked about it, her dad's face turned bright red.

Gina and Darris decided to spend their time together in Manchester. Gina wanted to get a Saturday job so she could help him buy his train tickets.

They talked about school too. Both planned to work really hard to get good GCSE results. And then they wanted to study sport at college. Maybe Darris could come to live in Manchester – or Gina could move to London. Who knew?

"Love's young dream!" laughed Grandma in the kitchen as she cut her wonderful homemade chocolate cake. She put the cake on plates, and I carried them into the living room.

I knew that Grandma still felt a bit funny about what had happened. She liked Gina, and she had almost managed to forgive her dad, but she was an old lady and for her things couldn't go back to normal so quickly. She followed me into the living room and sat down in her favourite chair.

She looked at Gina and Darris for a few seconds before she said, "So Gina. Will you look after my favourite grandson?"

"Of course," smiled Gina. "And he'll look after me."

Chapter 26 Thursday, January 26th – Gina

The school hall was packed. I looked down at the pupils from the stage. Hundreds of faces stared back at me. The principal started to speak. "This morning we're going to hear the winning story from the writing competition. Congratulations, Gina Ward."

I stood up and walked nervously to the microphone. I breathed deeply and started to read.

My proud people

What do you see? You see people living in caravans. Gypsies, Travellers – you think we're all the same. But we're not. Gypsies came originally from India. And Irish Travellers? Guess what, we're from Ireland.

You see caravans on campsites. You think houses are better. We disagree. We love our caravans. We clean them from top to bottom every day. We love the freedom they give us. Our families can live side by side. Children can play safely. And we can go anywhere we want. Or can we?

You see the eviction of Travellers on the news. The police tell us we can't stay. But where can we go? There isn't enough land for Travellers. That's why some of us have to move into houses, though we don't always want to.

You see Traveller children playing truant. You ask, why aren't they at school? Because Traveller children have to go to new schools every time they move. New schools, new faces, endless bullying. That's why Traveller children stay away from school and don't get a good education.

You see Travellers who can't read. You think we're stupid. But we have our own language. It's called Shelta. It's a spoken, not a written language. We pass down our traditions through story-telling and song. In our culture we don't always use the written word because we don't need to.

So next time you walk past a Traveller caravan, think about what's inside. A clean, tidy, happy home. A home full of people who love and protect each other – full of music and stories and laughter. And most important of all: full of pride.

The pupils and teachers started to clap. Their applause seemed to last a long time. I was still breathing deeply and my hands were shaking, but that didn't matter. People had heard my story, and now they knew where I came from.

Chapter 27 Thursday, January 26th – Grace

School had finished for the day, and though the afternoon was freezing cold, the sun shone brightly. Gina and I looked at each other and smiled. She hugged her warm winter coat around her, and we strolled out of the school gates together.

All Gina's anxiety had gone. She was strong and confident now. She took my arm and, as we walked home in the winter sunlight, the future looked bright.

Vocabulary

Abbreviations
sb. = somebody; sth. = something;
Abk. = Abkürzung; Bez. = Bezeichnung; jmdm. = jemandem;
jmdn. = jemanden; umg. = umgangssprachlich

A

(to) **ache** [eɪk] wehtun, schmerzen
ackee [æki] Akee *(ein mit der Litchi verwandtes Seifenbaumgewächs)*
aged [eɪdʒd] im Alter von … Jahren
air [eə] Luft; *Bez. für einen speziellen Skateboardsprung*
allowed [ə'laʊd]: (to) **be allowed to do sth.** etwas tun dürfen
(to) **annoy** [ə'nɔɪ] ärgern
anxiety [æŋ'zaɪəti] Angst, Sorge
(to) **appreciate** [ə'priːʃieɪt] (wert)schätzen
(to) **arrange** [ə'reɪndʒ] arrangieren, planen
arrival [ə'raɪvl] Ankunft
ashamed [ə'ʃeɪmd]: (to) **be ashamed** sich schämen
asleep [ə'sliːp]: (to) **be asleep** schlafen
ate [et]: (to) **eat** [iːt] essen **(eat, ate, eaten)**
attacker [ə'tækə] Angreifer
attitude ['ætɪtjuːd] Einstellung
(to) **avoid** [ə'vɔɪd] vermeiden

B

bacon ['beɪkən] (Schinken)speck
(to) **bang** [bæŋ] (zusammen)stoßen
(to) **beam** [biːm] strahlen
(to) **bear** [beə] ertragen
(to) **behave** [bɪ'heɪv] sich benehmen
bite [baɪt] Bissen; Happen
black eye [ˌblæk'aɪ] blaues Auge
Bonfire Night ['bɒnfaɪə naɪt] *Abend des 5. November, an dem Feuerwerke und Freudenfeuer zum Gedenken an die Pulververschwörung im Jahre 1605 in Großbritannien veranstaltet werden*
both [bəʊθ] beide
bracelet ['breɪslət] Armband
(to) **breathe** [briːð] atmen
bright [braɪt] leuchtend; strahlend
bucket ['bʌkɪt] Eimer
(to) **build** [bɪld] bauen
burnt [bɜːnt] angebrannt; verbrannt

C

(to) **call** [kɔːl] rufen; anrufen
campsite ['kæmpsaɪt] Campingplatz
caravan site ['kærəvæn'saɪt] Stellplatz *(für Wohnwagen)*
(to) **care** [keə] sich kümmern
carpet ['kɑːpɪt] Teppich
(to) **carry on** [ˌkæri'ɒn] weitermachen
(to) **catch up** [ˌkætʃ'ʌp] einholen
(to) **cause** [kɔːz] bereiten; verursachen
(to) **celebrate** ['selɪbreɪt] feiern
century ['sentʃəri] Jahrhundert
changing room ['tʃeɪndʒɪŋ ruːm] Umkleidekabine
cheque [tʃek] Scheck
(to) **chew** [tʃuː] kauen
choice [tʃɔɪs] (Aus)wahl
(to) **choose** [tʃuːz] (aus)wählen, aussuchen
Christmas Eve [ˌkrɪsməs'iːv] Heiligabend
(to) **clap** [klæp] klatschen
claustrophobic [ˌklɔːstrə'fəʊbɪk]: (to) **feel claustrophobic** sich eingeengt fühlen
cloth [klɒθ] Putzlappen; Stoff
coat [kəʊt] Mantel
common ['kɒmən]: (to) **have sth. in common** etwas gemeinsam haben
community [kə'mjuːnəti] Gemeinschaft, Gemeinde
confident ['kɒnfɪdənt] zuversichtlich, selbstsicher
confused [kən'fjuːzd] verwirrt
cooker ['kʊkə] Herd
corner ['kɔːnə] Ecke
council ['kaʊnsl] Stadtrat
couple ['kʌpl] Paar
covered ['kʌvəd] bedeckt
cracked rib [krækt'rɪb] angebrochene Rippe
crept [krept]: (to) creep [kriːp] schleichen **(creep, crept, crept)**
crossed [krɒst] verschränkt
crossly ['krɒsli] verärgert
crowd [kraʊd] Menschenmenge; Zuschauer
crowded ['kraʊdɪd] überfüllt
crush [krʌʃ]: (to) **have a crush on sb.** in jmdn. verknallt sein
cubicle ['kjuːbɪkl] (Toiletten)kabine
curiously ['kjʊəriəsli] neugierig
cushion ['kʊʃn] Kissen

D

(to) **decide** [dɪ'saɪd] beschließen, (sich) entscheiden
(to) **decorate** ['dekəreɪt] schmücken; verzieren
deeply [diːpli] tief
degree [dɪ'griː] Grad
(to) **deserve** [dɪ'zɜːv] verdienen
determined [dɪ'tɜːmɪnd] entschlossen
(to) **develop** [dɪ'veləp] (sich) entwickeln
(to) **disagree** [ˌdɪsə'griː] anderer Meinung sein

(to) **disappear** [ˌdɪsə'pɪə] verschwinden
(to) **do well** [duː'wel] gut abschneiden
doll [dɒl] Puppe
doorway ['dɔːweɪ] Eingang, Tür
downstairs [ˌdaʊn'steəz] unten, im unteren Stockwerk
(to) **drop** [drɒp] fallen

E

earphones ['ɪəfəʊnz] Kopfhörer
earring ['ɪərɪŋ] Ohrring
embarrassment [ɪm'bærəsmənt] Verlegenheit
engaged [ɪn'geɪdʒd]: (to) **be engaged** verlobt sein
(to) **enjoy** [ɪn'dʒɔɪ] genießen, etwas gerne tun
(to) **enter** ['entə] eintreten; teilnehmen; sich beteiligen
envelope ['envələʊp] Umschlag
equipment [ɪ'kwɪpmənt] Ausrüstung
ethnic minority ['eθnɪk maɪ'nɒrəti] ethnische Minderheit
eviction [ɪ'vɪkʃn] Zwangsräumung
excited [ɪk'saɪtɪd] aufgeregt
exhausted [ɪg'zɔːstɪd] erschöpft

F

fault [fɔːlt] Schuld, Fehler
feeling ['fiːlɪŋ] Gefühl
few [fjuː]: **a few** ein paar
fiancé [fi'ɒnseɪ] Verlobter
(to) **fight** [faɪt] kämpfen
firework display ['faɪəwɜːk dɪ'spleɪ] Feuerwerk
flew out [ˌfluː'aʊt]: (to) **fly out** [ˌflaɪ'aʊt] herausfliegen **(fly, flew, flown)**
flight [flaɪt] Flug
fond [fɒnd]: (to) **be fond of sb.** jmdn. gernhaben
(to) **forgive** [fə'gɪv] vergeben, verzeihen
frail [freɪl] schwach; zerbrechlich
freezing cold ['friːzɪŋ kəʊld] eiskalt
front door [frʌnt dɔː] Haustür
frown [fraʊn] die Stirn runzeln
furiously ['fjʊəriəsli] wütend

G

gap [gæp] Lücke
GCSE [ˌdʒiːsiːes'iː] General Certificate of Secondary Education *(Schulabschluss im britischen Schulsystem)*
gently ['dʒentli] sanft
(to) **get away** [ˌgetə'weɪ] verschwinden
(to) **get out** [ˌget'aʊt] aussteigen; herauskommen
gift [gɪft] Geschenk
glare [gleə]: (to) **glare at sb.** jmdm. einen wütenden Blick zuwerfen
glasses ['glɑːsɪz]: **pair of glasses** Brille
gone [gɒn]: (to) **go** [gəʊ] gehen **(go, went, gone)**

good-looking [ˌgʊdˈlʊkɪŋ] gut aussehend
grandson [ˈgrænsʌn] Enkel
grew wider [gruːˈwaɪdə]: (to) **grow wider** [grəʊˈwaɪdə] breiter werden **(grow, grew, grown)**
grin [grɪn] Grinsen
grumpy [ˈgrʌmpi] schlecht gelaunt, mürrisch
Gypsy [ˈdʒɪpsi] *Angehörige(r) der Gruppe der Roma*

H

hoity-toity [ˌhɔɪtiˈtɔɪti] *abwertend* eingebildet
(to) **hug** [hʌg] umarmen
(to) **hug a coat around sb.** jmdn. in einen Mantel mummeln
hung [hʌŋ]: (to) **hang** [hæŋ] (auf)hängen **(hang, hung, hung)**
husband [ˈhʌzbənd] Ehemann

I

immediately [ɪˈmiːdiətli] sofort
impressed [ɪmˈprest] beeindruckt
injury [ˈɪndʒəri] Verletzung
(to) **introduce** [ˌɪntrəˈdjuːs] (sich) vorstellen
involved [ɪnˈvɒlvd]: (to) **get involved** sich einlassen; verwickelt werden
(to) **iron** [ˈaɪən] bügeln

K

(to) **kick** [kɪk] treten
(to) **kneel** [niːl] knien
(to) **knock** [nɒk] klopfen
knock [nɒk] Klopfen

L

(to) **laugh at** [ˈlɑːf ət] auslachen
laughter [ˈlɑːftə] Lachen
(to) **lean against** sth. [ˌliːnəˈgenst] lehnen an …, sich anlehnen an …
leg [leg] Bein
linger [ˈlɪŋgə]: (to) **linger in the air** in der Luft liegen
lively [ˈlaɪvli] lebendig; lebhaft
(to) **look around** [ˌlʊkəˈraʊnd] sich umsehen

M

(to) **manage** [ˈmænɪdʒ] (etwas) schaffen
(to) **march** [mɑːtʃ] marschieren
married [ˈmærid]: (to) **get married** heiraten
(to) **matter** [ˈmætə] wichtig sein
meal [miːl] Mahlzeit, Essen
mood [muːd] Stimmung
movement [ˈmuːvmənt] Bewegung

N

noisy [ˈnɔɪzi] laut

O

occasionally [ə'keɪʒnəli] gelegentlich
oi [ɔɪ] *umg.* he
old-fashioned [ˌəʊld'fæʃnd] altmodisch
(to) **ooh and aah** [uːənd'aː] *umg.* staunen
otherwise ['ʌðəwaɪz] ansonsten

P

painful ['peɪnfl] schmerzhaft
(to) **pass down** [ˌpɑːs'daʊn] weitergeben; überliefern
piece [piːs]: **a piece of paper** ein Blatt Papier
pikey ['paɪki] *Schimpfwort* → Traveller, Gypsy
plate [pleɪt] Teller
pleased [pliːzd]: (to) **be pleased** zufrieden sein
(to) **point** [pɔɪnt] zeigen
ponytail ['pəʊnɪteɪl] Pferdeschwanz
possessively [pə'zesɪvli] besitzergreifend
(to) **prepare** [prɪ'peə] vorbereiten
pretty ['prɪti] hübsch
pride [praɪd] Stolz
principal ['prɪnsəpl] Rektor(in)
privacy ['prɪvəsi] Privatsphäre
(to) **protect** [prə'tekt] schützen
(to) **pull out** [ˌpʊl'aʊt] (heraus) ziehen
pushchair ['pʊʃtʃeə] Buggy, Kinderwagen
(to) **put down** [ˌpʊt'daʊn] weglegen

R

racism ['reɪsɪzəm] Rassimus
racist ['reɪsɪst] rassistisch
(to) **raise** [reɪz] heben
ramp [ræmp] Rampe
reason ['riːzn] Grund
(to) **recognize** ['rekəgnaɪz] erkennen
relationship [rɪ'leɪʃnʃɪp] Beziehung
relaxation [ˌriːlæk'seɪʃn] Entspannung
relief [rɪ'liːf] Erleichterung
(to) **remain** [rɪ'meɪn] (übrig) bleiben
remote control [rɪˌməʊt kən'trəʊl] Fernbedienung
(to) **reply** [rɪ'plaɪ] antworten, erwidern
reputation [ˌrepju'teɪʃn]: (to) **have a bad reputation** einen schlechten Ruf haben
(to) **return** [rɪ'tɜːn] zurückkehren, zurückkommen
(to) **rinse** [rɪns] spülen
round [raʊnd] Runde
row [rəʊ] Reihe; Streit
rubbish ['rʌbɪʃ] Abfall, Müll
(to) **rush** [rʌʃ] hasten

S

(to) **scatter** ['skætə] (ver)streuen
secret ['siːkrət]: **in secret** heimlich, im Geheimen
serious ['sɪəriəs] ernst, ernsthaft
shape [ʃeɪp] Form

sharp pain [ʃɑːp peɪn] stechender Schmerz

shone [ʃɒn]: (to) **shine** [ʃaɪn] scheinen **(shine, shone, shone)**

shout [ʃaʊt]: (to) **shout at sb.** jmdn. anschreien

(to) **sigh** [saɪ] seufzen

(to) **sneer** [snɪə] höhnisch grinsen

sky [skaɪ] Himmel

smell [smel] Geruch

(to) **snap** [snæp] ausrasten (to) **snap at sb.** jmdn. anschnauzen

son [sʌn] Sohn

(to) **solve** [sɒlv] lösen

sore [sɔː]: **still a bit sore** noch nicht ganz gesund

spicy ['spaɪsi] würzig

(to) **split up** [ˌsplɪt'ʌp] sich trennen

spoke [spəʊk]: (to) **speak** [spiːk] sprechen **(speak, spoke, spoken)**

spun around [spʌnə'raʊnd]: (to) **spin around** [spɪn ə'raʊnd] (sich) schnell drehen **(spin, spun, spun)**

stage [steɪdʒ] Bühne

stairs [steəs] Treppe

(to) **stammer** ['stæmə] stottern, stammeln

(to) **stare at** ['steər ət] anstarren

stocking ['stɒkɪŋ] Strumpf

stood [stʊd]: (to) **stand** [stænd] stehen **(stand, stood, stood)**

storytelling ['stɔːritelɪŋ] Geschichtenerzählen

(to) **stroll** [strəʊl] bummeln, schlendern

strong [strɒŋ] stark

(to) **study** ['stʌdi] studieren; lernen

successful [sək'sesfl] erfolgreich

sulkily ['sʌlkɪili] eingeschnappt, schmollend

swollen ['swəʊlən] geschwollen

T

(to) **taste** [teɪst] schmecken; kosten

taught [tɔːt]: (to) **teach** [tiːtʃ] beibringen **(teach, taught, taught)**

term [tɜːm] Schul(halb)jahr

(to) **text** [tekst] eine SMS senden

though [ðəʊ] obwohl

threw [θruː]: (to) **throw** [θrəʊ] werfen **(throw, threw, thrown)**

tidy ['taɪdi] ordentlich

toddler ['tɒdlə] Kleinkind

tomboy ['tɒmbɔɪ] Wildfang

towel ['taʊəl] Handtuch

Traveller ['trævələ]: **Irish Traveller** *meist nomadisch lebende ethnische Gruppe, die ihre Wurzeln in Irland hat*

truant ['truːənt]: (to) **play truant** die Schule schwänzen

(to) try on [ˌtraɪˈɒn]
anprobieren

U

UK [ˌjuːˈkeɪ] *Abk.* Großbritannien *(Vereinigtes Königreich von Großbritannien und Nordirland)*

unavoidable [ˌʌnəˈvɔɪdəbl]
unvermeidlich

upset [ʌpˈset] betrübt

V

victim [ˈvɪktɪm] Opfer

voice [vɔɪs] Stimme

W

wall [wɔːl]: **freshly painted wall**
frisch gestrichende Wand

(to) wave at sb. [ˈweɪv ət]
jmdm. zuwinken

(to) whisper [ˈwɪspə] flüstern

whole [həʊl]: **the whole world**
die ganze Welt

wife [waɪf] Ehefrau

wintry [ˈwɪntri] winterlich

wisely [ˈwaɪzli] klug; wohl überlegt

woke up [wəʊkˈʌp]: (to) **wake up** [ˌweɪkˈʌp] aufwachen **(wake, woke, woken)**

(to) wonder [ˈwʌndə]
sich fragen

wrapping paper [ˈræpɪŋ peɪpə]
Geschenkpapier

Y

yard [jɑːd] *Maßeinheit*
1 Yard = 0,9144 m

(to) yawn [jɔːn] gähnen

Check your understanding

Chapter 1

1 How did Gina and Grace get home after school?

2 What was Gina not allowed to wear at school?

Chapter 2

1 Why did Gina and her family often move in Ireland?

2 What happened to Gina in the playground after school?

Chapter 3

1 What were Grace's and Darris' plans for the weekend?

2 When did Gina have to be home from the disco?

Chapter 4

1 What did Grace and Darris learn about Irish Travellers?

Chapter 5

1 How did Gina describe Robert?

2 What did Gina's dad say to Darris?

Chapter 6

1 What happened to Darris in the second round of the competition?

Chapter 7

1 What did Grace, her mum, her grandma and Darris do on Bonfire Night?

Chapter 8

1 What were Gina and her mum talking about in the kitchen?

Chapter 9

1 How did Darris describe Brixton in his e-mail?

Chapter 10

1 Gina needs help. How can Grace help her?

Chapter 11

1 How did Grace earn some money for shopping?
2 What did Gina, Rosie and Grace buy?

Chapter 12

1 What competition will Gina enter at school?
2 How did Grace and Gina spend Christmas?

Chapter 13

1 What did Gina do on this Saturday morning?
2 Who came around for a cup of tea?

Chapter 14

1 What news did Darris get? How did he feel?

Chapter 15

1 What happened in the night of December 23rd?

Chapter 16

1 What did Gina's dad and Robert do?

Chapter 17

1 What things were important to Gina?

Chapter 18

1 How did Darris' family spend Christmas morning?

Chapter 19

1 How did Gina's mum feel about their visitors?

Chapter 20

1 Where did Darris and his family go to?
2 What happened in the park?

Chapter 21

1 Who remembered every detail of the things that had happened in the park?
2 Why was Gina ashamed when she was alone with her mum?

Chapter 22

1 When did Gina leave the hospital?

Chapter 23

1 What did Gina's mum say when Robert called Darris an idiot?

Chapter 24

1 Why did Gina's dad go to Darris and what did he say to Darris?

Chapter 25

1 What were Darris' and Gina's plans for the future?

Chapter 26

1 What was Gina's story about?
2 What was the school's reaction when Gina had finished reading her story?

Chapter 27

1 How did Gina feel?